THE TRACTARIANS AND ROMAN CATHOLICISM

OXFORD MOVEMENT CENTENARY SERIES

THE TRACTARIANS AND ROMAN CATHOLICISM

BY

F. L. CROSS, M.A., D.Phil.

LIBRARIAN OF PUSEY HOUSE, OXFORD,
AND EXAMINING CHAPLAIN TO THE LORD BISHOP OF BRADFORD

WIPF & STOCK · Eugene, Oregon

Wipf and Stock Publishers
199 W 8th Ave, Suite 3
Eugene, OR 97401

The Tractarians and Roman Catholicism
By Cross, Frank Leslie
ISBN 13: 978-1-62032-348-9
Publication date 7/15/2012
Previously published by SPCK, 1933

This is one of a series approved by the Literature Committee of the Oxford Movement Centenary Committee appointed by the Archbishops of Canterbury and York.

CONTENTS

PREFACE

Until quite recent times the opinion was widely voiced—and even today it is occasionally met with—that the chief end of the Oxford Movement was to Romanize the Church of England. The object of the present study is to show how completely such an opinion is at variance with the facts. In its pages a number of passages will be recalled from Tractarian writings which condemn Roman Catholicism in the fiercest terms, and some of these passages cannot but seem too combative in an age which has learnt to discuss differences of principle in a more Christian temper. The violence of some of Newman's polemical writings against Rome during the early years of the Oxford Movement will probably surprise those who have never been led to trace out his remarks on the subject. It may, therefore, be as well to state that these pages have been written with purely historical motives, and certainly not in order to advocate the revival of such language about the Church of Rome as was all but universal in the Church of England a century ago.

The writer desires to express his sincere thanks to the Reverend Canon S. L. Ollard, who has assisted him unsparingly with his unique knowledge of the Movement; to the Principal of St. Edmund Hall, Oxford; to the Reverend the Principal of Pusey House, Oxford; and to the Reverend E. Marsh for help in connexion with the present study.

F. L. C.

Feast of St. Benedict, 1933.

CHAPTER I

In 1829, Parliament passed the Act of Catholic Emancipation, a measure which was long overdue. After 1745, the Jacobites had ceased to be a menace to the Crown, and justice demanded that the toleration granted to Nonconformists in 1689 should be extended also to Roman Catholics. But fears of " Popery " were deeply rooted in the nation, and successive Governments feared to act. When in 1778 some measure of alleviation had been granted to the Papists, the Gordon Riots of 1780 had indicated how such alleviation was regarded by a section at least of the population. When, however, half a century later, in 1828, the repeal of the Test and Corporation Acts removed the last disabilities of Nonconforming Protestants, relief to the Roman Catholics could no longer be denied.

The battle was a fierce one in its last stages. After having convinced the Duke of Wellington of the need for Emancipation, Peel made himself responsible for the measure in the House of Commons. Since 1817, Peel had been one of the Burgesses for Oxford University. At the time of his election he was strongly opposed to Emancipation, and the Tory Party had refused to allow Canning to be nominated on the ground of his pro-Catholic sympathies. In 1829, therefore,

Peel " felt bound to surrender to the University without delay the trust " confided to him, and resigned.   When he sought re-election, a violent contest ensued, and in the event Peel lost his seat to Sir Robert Inglis; he had to content himself with the pocket-borough of Westbury, to which he was elected shortly afterwards.   It is interesting to note that in the contest Pusey supported Peel, while Newman opposed him.

Through this contest Roman Catholicism had been brought prominently before the eyes of the University in 1830.   But it came before it as an idea rather than as an institution.   The University still required all its members to subscribe to the Thirty-nine Articles, and thus excluded Roman Catholics as well as Dissenters from its life.   There were, it is true, relatively very few Roman Catholics in England at this time.   We know that several became Anglicans towards the end of the preceding century.   And among those who continued to hold to their faith, a tradition had grown up which led them to isolate themselves from taking such part in the national life as the Penal Laws allowed them.   The manner in which these laws had been administered further fostered this temper of aloofness.   As long as Roman Catholics were content to practise their religion unobtrusively, the authorities normally kept the laws against them in suspense.   The majority of their adherents were either members of old Roman Catholic families, who had their own chapels in remote country mansions, or else attached to the foreign embassies in London. Accordingly, Roman Catholics were but rarely met with by the normal Englishman.   Since the later years of the Eighteenth Century, there had existed in Oxford a small Roman Catholic Chapel in the part of the city beyond Magdalen Bridge known as St. Clement's. Newman, it is said, claimed the priest as a parishioner when he was a curate of the old St. Clement's Church. But there is no evidence that any of the Tractarians ever entered this chapel. Of Roman Catholicism in England most of them had no practical knowledge at all.[1]

Consequently, in Tractarian times, the conception of Roman Catholicism generally current was derived not from actual contact with English Romanism, but principally from two other sources. The one was the much read commentaries on the Books of *Daniel* and *Revelation*. The other was from what was seen of Roman Catholicism on the Continent.

Before the rise of modern Biblical criticism, the imagery and prophecies of *Daniel* and *Revelation* were interpreted as pointing explicitly and in detail to the history of later ages, and Protestant commentators regularly identified the visions of the Beast and of Babylon and of the Scarlet Woman with the Papacy. The investigation of the meaning of each piece of symbolism gave ample opportunity for disserting on Rome. Illustrations and anecdotes were introduced in abundance in order to show the iniquities of the Roman Catholic Church in history and in experience. The

---

[1] On the condition of Roman Catholicism in the Eighteenth and early Nineteenth Centuries, see E. Burton, *Life of Bishop Challoner*, and the extended treatment of the subject in Dr. Bernard Ward's series of volumes on the period preceding Emancipation. On the Chapel in St. Clement's at Oxford, see Peter Maurice, *Popery in Oxford* (1832). A most valuable account of the state of Roman Catholicism in the diocese of York in the middle of the Eighteenth Century, by Canon S. L. Ollard, will be found in the *Record Series* of the Yorkshire Archaeological Society, vol. 77 (1930), pp. 186-222. It is based on Archbishop Herring's Visitation Returns for 1743.

wide circulation which such commentaries enjoyed was undoubtedly largely responsible for the popular view of Roman Catholicism held a century ago.

The second influence in moulding the conception of Rome was scarcely more in her favour—namely, the contacts gained by travellers with Roman Catholicism on the Continent. Englishmen took abroad with them their own ideas of religion, and when they visited Roman Catholic churches they saw much that savoured of superstition. The idolatry which *Daniel* and *Revelation* had foretold could now be seen in actual life. Peasants were to be seen praying to statues, and kissing relics, and worshipping the Host. Stories of the iniquities of the *curia* and the immorality of the priesthood were seized upon and widely circulated by those searching for scandal. Even when prejudice had been set aside, there was a great deal, and always will be, in continental Roman Catholic worship repellent to English tastes. Newman and Froude were disgusted with what they saw in Mediterranean regions. Only those such as Manning, who were already temperamentally disposed in favour of Rome, told a different tale when they came home.

With the Roman Catholic treatises of controversial theology the Tractarians had little first-hand acquaintance. William Palmer, as will be seen below, had studied the controversy in its primary sources (*e.g.*, in Bellarmine); the others were, however, familiar with it in excellent second-hand sources—namely, in the Seventeenth-Century Anglican divines.

Such, in very brief outline, were the nature and sources of the conception of Roman Catholicism current a century ago.

CHAPTER II

THE very varied ancestry of the leaders of the Oxford Movement was reflected in their widely differing attitudes towards the Church of Rome. In the present chapter we shall examine briefly these differences, particularly as they were exemplified in the first four years of the Movement (1833-1836). The evidence of the *Tracts* themselves will be reserved for the next chapter. The position of Hurrell Froude will be discussed in connexion with his *Remains* in Chapter VI.

WILLIAM PALMER

One of the most learned of the original leaders of the Oxford Movement was William Palmer of Worcester College (not to be confused with his namesake of Magdalen). Born in 1803, he was slightly younger than Pusey and Newman. In 1832 he published his *Origines Liturgicæ*, which to the learned world was a testimony of his erudition. By tradition a member of the old High Church School, he remained such to the end of his life. He was violently opposed to the "reforming" measures of the time and, like most High Churchmen, strongly disapproved of Catholic Emancipation. He referred to the Emancipation Act as " a measure which scattered to the winds public principle, public morality, public confidence, and dispersed a party which, had it possessed courage to adhere to its old and popular principles, and to act on them with manly energy, would have stemmed the torrent of revolution, and averted the awful crisis which was at hand " (*Narrative of Events*, 1843, p. 96). He was one of those who attended the conference arranged by Rose at the Rectory at Hadleigh in July, 1832, and he was mainly responsible for the two Addresses which were presented in 1834 to the Archbishop by the clergy and laity respectively, proclaiming the rally to the Church. In 1838 Palmer published two volumes of monumental learning on *The Church of Christ,* where he defended the strictly " High Anglican " position. *Tract No.* 15 was the working over of some of his notes by Newman; but otherwise he did not contribute to the *Tracts for the Times.* From the outset, he had desired the formation of a society in defence of Church principles rather than propaganda by tracts, and this fact partly explains why he did not take a larger share in them. When, however, in 1841 *Tract No.* 90 was condemned, Palmer came forward nobly in support of its author. This was a generous action on his part, for latterly he had been on the whole far more conservative than Newman.

Of the Tractarians, Palmer was certainly the most well versed in the Roman controversy. Perrone, the Jesuit theologian at Rome and, later, friend of Newman, described him as *theologorum Oxoniensium facile princeps.* Palmer had not the philosophical mind of Newman, and could never have treated the issue in the manner of Newman's *Lectures on the Prophetical Office.* But, unlike most of the Tractarians, he was familiar at first hand with the Roman case as expounded by Bellarmine and other leading Roman Catholic controversialists. In his *Treatise on the Church* he was led to expound his attitude to Rome in some detail.

Where in the *Treatise* Palmer dealt theologically with the Roman Church, he defended the usual High Anglican position. As against many of the Reformers, he held that the Roman Church continued to be part of the Church of Christ up to the Reformation (I. xi. § 1). Even the post-Reformation Roman Catholic Church was still part of the true Church; as the Seventeenth-Century theologians would have put it, she had not erred on "fundamentals." "To me it appears infinitely safer and more charitable to prefer the opinion of the majority of theologians, who consider the Roman Churches, though in several respects faulty and corrupted in doctrine and discipline, yet still to continue a portion of the Catholic Church of Christ" (i. 282 *f*.). This position is defended by the usual arguments.

Yet Palmer had no doubt as to the grave errors into which Rome in practice had fallen. "To those who are acquainted with the history of the Roman Churches, in connexion with Jansenism, few things can appear more absurd than the air of triumph with which modern Romish theologians vaunt the *unity* of their Church in *faith*, its sole and exclusive possession of authority for the *termination of religious controversies*, and its freedom from all *heresy*" (i. 318 *f*.). The first volume contains an Appendix (II., pp. 344 *f*.) entitled "On Infidelity and Indifference in the Roman Church," of which the following extract is typical: "It is a certain fact that many of the worst infidels of the last century were members of the Roman Church, that they received its sacraments, and even officiated as ministers at its altars " (p. 345).

In 1843, when (as we shall see) the accusation of " Romanizing " could be made with some justice against a section of the Oxford leaders, Palmer published his *Narrative of Events* in order to prove that such Romanizing was foreign to the original aims of the Movement, and also to voice his own dissent from those who now held " Romanizing " views. Referring to the Association in defence of the Church formed a decade earlier, he pointed out that it was instituted with the purpose of supporting the Church of England " against its opponents, whether Romanists, Dissenters, or Rationalists " (p. 106). The events connected with the Association were recalled in some detail; and Palmer summed up by saying that he believed that his account would exculpate those who signed it " from any imputation of designs hostile to the doctrines or discipline of the Church of England, or favourable to the introduction of Romanism " (p. 117). No less convinced was he that the *Tracts* themselves were hostile to Romanism. On page 143 he wrote, " I have no hesitation in saying that a candid examination of the greater part of the *Tracts for the Times* and of the writings of their authors will sufficiently prove that (whatever may be thought of their individual opinions on particular points) there is throughout a continual avowal of *opposition to Rome in general*,[1] a strong sense of its corruptions and errors, an earnest wish to resist those errors."

Palmer, therefore, while not going as far as those theologians who denied that Rome as she now is can

[1] Author's italics.

still be reckoned a part of the Church of Christ, vigorously asserted her doctrinal errors and moral imperfections. He believed that the Oxford Movement was but reiterating the traditional Anglican High Church teaching on the Roman issue.

EDWARD BOUVERIE PUSEY

Unlike Palmer, Pusey had not been brought up a strict High Churchman. Though from childhood deeply religious and serious by temperament, he probably attached little importance to ecclesiastical questions as a young man. After a brilliant career at the University, Pusey went to Germany, where he spent some two years. Here he could no longer avoid the ecclesiastical issue, and for a time was influenced by German liberalism. In 1825, Hugh James Rose, a High Churchman of Cambridge, wrote an attack on the liberalizing tendencies of German theology; and when Pusey had returned to England, he took up his pen in defence of German thought. His *Historical Enquiry into the Causes of the Rationalist Character lately Predominant in the Theology of Germany* appeared in two parts, in 1828 and 1830 respectively. It was a rather badly composed treatise, and Pusey later regretted the theological views it defended. But it gave him a theological label at the time, and in the early thirties Pusey was generally regarded in Oxford as a liberal theologian, though a man of deep piety and profound learning. Only in the last weeks of 1833 did he first associate himself with the Tractarians; and not till 1836 did he throw himself heart and soul into the Movement.

In estimating Pusey's attitude to Rome, we must

remember the respect in which he held the English Reformers of the Sixteenth Century. Pusey never shared the desire of the majority of the Tractarians to depreciate their work. Like most moderate Church-men of the time, he looked back to the Sixteenth Century as among the glories of the English Church, and it is very probable that his studies in Germany confirmed such views in him. In German Protestant theology the teaching of Luther occupies a position hardly second to that of St. Paul, and openly to disavow Luther in any major matter is to be guilty of heresy. Moreover, the infiltration of Catholic principles into German Protestant thought is almost prevented by the method in which the faculties are organized. Catholic and Protestant theologians are isolated by tradition, even though both faculties may co-exist in the same University. There is not (I believe) a single reference in Pusey's *Life* to his coming into contact with the Catholic theologians while he was in Germany, though at Bonn, where he studied, the two faculties—Catholic and Protestant—both existed. Pusey became so deeply imbued with respect for the Reformation that he was never able to regard it, as Newman and Keble did, as a mere incident in English Church history.

Pusey's more favourable attitude to the Reformers is also illustrated by his willingness at the outset to support the scheme for the Martyrs' Memorial in Oxford in 1838. It is true that he soon withdrew in order to avoid any open difference of opinion in the Tractarian ranks. But it is significant that his sympathy for the Reformation divines did not pre-vent him from entering whole-heartedly into the Tractarian battle, and in 1845, after Newman's secession, being immediately recognized as their natural leader.

Pusey's attitude to Rome is illustrated by a number of passages in the *Tracts* which will be quoted in the next chapter. It may be judged also from some passages which occur in a sermon that he preached before the University of Oxford on November 5, 1837, called " Patience and Confidence, the Strength of the Church." In this sermon he said: " From the time that the Church of Rome began to forsake the principles of the Church Catholic and grasp after human means, she began also to take evil means for good ends, and incurring the Apostolic curse on them who ' do evil that good may come,' took at last evil means for evil ends. She, the Apostolic Church of the West, consecrated by Apostolic blood, showed herself rather the descendant of them who slew the Apostles, and ' thought that they did God service,' stained herself with the blood of the saints, that on her might come all the righteous blood which was shed within her: even of the very Apostles, who had shed their blood for her. There is not an enormity which has been practised against people or kings by miscreants in the name of God, but the divines of that unhappy Church have abetted or justified " (pp. 27 *f.*) And again: " The principle of the Romish Church was expediency; it was a plotting, scheming, worldly spirit, having at first God's glory for its end, but seeking it by secular means, and at last, in punishment, left to seek its own glory, and to set itself up in the place of God " (p. 29).

When, from 1838 onwards, the allegations of " Popery " were beginning to be made constantly against Tractarianism, it was Pusey who in 1839 published a *Letter* to prove the falsity of the charge, and showed that " to oppose Ultra-Protestantism is not to favour Popery" (Title to Appendix). To this we shall return later.

JOHN KEBLE

Keble's attitude to Rome is less easy to discover. It is likely that he was never much concerned with the question. By tradition a High Churchman—less rigid perhaps than Palmer—and possessed of a great affection for the simple piety of the Seventeenth Century as expressed in George Herbert's *Poems*, Keble had by nature little sympathy with the Roman Catholic *ethos*. He never went abroad until the latter part of his life, and was therefore not introduced to Roman Catholicism in that way. In the face of so little evidence to show what Keble's attitude to Roman Catholicism was, perhaps it may be best described as that of tolerance towards an institution which he did not understand. It may be anticipated that Keble himself would have been little attracted towards Roman Catholic types of piety. Yet if he had been as strongly hostile to Rome as was Palmer, it is unlikely that he would have allowed Froude's *Remains* to contain their fiercely " anti-Reformation" passages, and identified himself with them later.

In the last lines on " The Gunpowder Treason " in the *Christian Year* (1827), Keble recognized that Rome had subtle attractions at least for some temperaments, and uttered a warning against the temptations to relapse to her fold. Moreover, in referring to Rome as " our sister " he clearly believed that she was a part of the Church. The lines in question are:

> " Thus, should thy soul misgiving turn
>   Back to th' enchanted air,
> Solace and warning thou mayst learn
>   From all that tempts thee there.
>
> " And O ! by all the pangs and fears
>   Fraternal spirits know,
> When for an elder's shame the tears
>   Of wakeful anguish flow,
>
> " Speak gently of our sister's fall;
>   Who knows but gentle love
> May win her at our patient call
>   The surer way to prove ?"

Where references to Rome occur in Keble's prose writings, he usually repeated the conventional language. For instance in the *Sermon on Primitive Tradition* (1836) he spoke of " the exorbitant claims of Rome," against which the Church of England had to be vindicated (p. 6); or, again, of " the undue claims and pernicious errors of Rome " (pp. 20 *f.*). In more than one passage in this *Sermon* Rome and Protestantism are brought into conjunction as containing opposing errors against which the Church had to guard herself and pursue what Newman described as the *Via Media*. Transubstantiation and the denial of the Real Presence in the Eucharist were both to be rejected, for both were " endeavours to explain away and bring nearer to the human intellect that which had been left thoroughly mysterious both by Scripture and Tradition " (p. 47). Again, " the Romanists make bold with the word Tradition," using it as a weapon to defend unhistorical doctrines; while Ultra-Protestants rely on Scripture alone (p. 147). In the Preface to the famous Assize Sermon, after deploring the interference of the legislature with the rights of the Church, he enquired: " What answer can we make henceforth to the partisans of the Bishop of Rome, when they taunt us with being a mere Parliamentarian Church?" (p. iv).

JOHN HENRY NEWMAN

Newman had a mind far less stable than that of the Tractarians whom we have so far considered. His tendency to be influenced by the ideas and circumstances of the moment was both his strength and his weakness. Before the Tractarian Movement began, he had already passed through several phases. Brought up in an Evangelical tradition, he underwent a conversion at school which influenced his whole life. For a period in the twenties he tended to a very different creed—the liberalism of the Noetics. At about the age of twenty-seven he was led back to a definitely orthodox creed, but this time with affinities to that of the old High Church school. A period of intensive study of the Fathers ensued, and in this way Newman became possessed of a high regard for the teachings of Antiquity; the fruit of it was a treatise entitled *The Arians of the Fourth Century*, which was finished in the summer of 1832 (though not published until the end of 1833).

It is not surprising that a mind which had already passed through many phases should have been less sure of its resting-place in the Roman issue than were those of Keble and Pusey and Palmer. In point of fact, Newman's attitude to Rome altered very considerably in the years from 1833 to 1845. Much more philosophical by nature than Pusey or Palmer, he treated the question in a different manner from them. He regarded it as a problem in the realm of ideas rather than in that of facts. Moreover, his extremely sensitive temperamental disposition led him to be influenced by what are commonly called psychological considerations to an extent altogether greater than the other leaders of the Movement.

In the early years of the Oxford Movement—and we will confine ourselves at present to these—Newman expressed himself in more vigorously anti-Roman terms than did the other leaders. Most of these utterances were in the *Tracts for the Times*, and of these a selection is printed in the next chapter. But they occurred frequently in his other writings too. In the *History of the Arians* he had said some hard things about Roman Catholicism; for example, he spoke of it as " the Papal Apostasy." In one of his articles on " Home Thoughts Abroad," which appeared in the *British Magazine* for February, 1834, Newman wrote the following words:

" The spirit of old Rome has risen again in its former place, and has evidenced its identity by its works. It has possessed the Church there planted, as an evil spirit might seize the demoniacs of primitive times and make her speak words which are not her own. In the corrupt Papal system, we have the very cruelty, the craft, and the ambition of the Republic; its cruelty in its unsparing sacrifice of the happiness and virtue of individuals to a phantom of public expediency, in its forced celibacy within, and its persecutions without; its craft in its falsehoods, its deceitful deeds, its lying wonders; and its grasping ambition in the very structure of its policy, in its assumption of universal dominion. Old Rome is still alive. Nowhere have its eagles lighted, but it still claims the sovereignty under another pretence. . . . The Roman Church I will not blame, but pity; she is, as I have said, spellbound, as if by an evil spirit; she is in thraldom " (pp. 123 f.).

Later in the article Newman admitted that the Church of Rome was not actually Anti-Christ (as many of the Evangelical divines of the time contended). But he had no doubt that she was fully infected with the Spirit of Anti-Christ; and continued:

" In the Book of Revelation, the sorceress upon the seven hills is not the *Church* of Rome, as is often taken for granted, but Rome itself, that bad spirit which, in its former shape, was the animating spirit of the Fourth Monarchy, and now has learned, by experience, a deeper cunning. In St. Paul's prophecy, it is not the *Temple* or *Church of God*, but the man of sin *in* the Temple, the old man or evil principle of the flesh, which exalteth itself against God. . . . Certainly it *is* a mystery of iniquity, and one which may well excite our dismay and horror, that in the very heart of the Church, in her highest dignity, in the seat of St. Peter, the evil spirit has throned itself, and rules. It seems as if that spirit had gained subtilty by years; Popish Rome has succeeded to Rome Pagan; and would that we had no reason to expect still more crafty developments of Anti-Christ amid the wreck of institutions and establishments which will attend the fall of the Papacy ! . . . I deny that the distinction is unmeaning. Is it nothing to be able to look on our Mother, to whom we owe the blessing of Christianity, with affection instead of hatred, with pity indeed, nay and fear, but not with horror ? . . . Is it nothing to rescue her from the hard names which interpreters of prophecy have put upon her, as an idolatress and an enemy of God, when she is deceived rather than a deceiver ?" (pp. 124 f.).

Rome was thus freed from the accusation of being herself Anti-Christ. But Satan dwelt securely within her fold. In Newman's *Sermons* there are also a number of passages in which reference is made to the sway which Satan held over the Roman Catholic Church. In the *Lectures on the Prophetical Office of the Church* the polemic against Rome reached its climax. But to the consideration of this we shall return in Chapter V.

ARTHUR PHILIP PERCEVAL

Perceval, who was a Chaplain to the King and is described by Newman as coming from the " Tory aristocracy," was more sympathetic in his attitude to Rome than most of the original Tractarians. He laid great emphasis upon the need for Apostolical Succession, and believed strongly in the " Branch Theory " of the Church. In his *Collection of Papers* (1843) he quoted with approval passages from letters in which his correspondents expressed their belief that Rome was certainly part of the Church. Thus Dr. James Walker, Bishop of Edinburgh, wrote to him on July 16, 1833: " I have long and much wished for a more intimate union among the different Churches which are subject to the primitive rule; and were such a happy union, by God's blessing, happily effected, I doubt not but that it would influence, not only the Dissenters, but portions at least, and ultimately perhaps large portions, of the Greek and Roman Churches. From the life of De Ricci, Bishop of Pistoia, we may perceive how easily, in happier circumstances, a reformation may be accomplished, in portions, at least, of the Roman Church " (p. 23).

Perceval also quoted a letter of Alexander Jolly,

dated September 7, 1829: " I do sadly lament the un-
Christian manner, so devoid of the primary requisites,
meekness and humility, in which controversy has been
too generally conducted, and that with the Church of
Rome in particular.   The gross mis-statements of its
antagonists, with the virulence of their writings, have
given great advantage to the Romanists.   The truth
we are commanded to speak in love; that we may grow
up into Him who is the Head, and by His influence be
attracted to coalesce in unity of spirit by the bond of
peace.   Many are the pathetic prayers and supplica-
tions presented in the use of our excellent Liturgy for
such harmonious peace and unity among those who
profess and call themselves Christians " (pp. 48 f.).

Both these letters, it will be noticed, date from pre-
Tractarian times.   The fact that Perceval quoted them
with approval is an indication of his own attitude
towards Rome.   The desire for reunion with Rome
expressed in them anticipated the feelings of the
" Romanizing " party, represented at a much later date
by Ward and Oakeley.

One point should be noticed in conclusion. It
probably hardly entered anyone's head at the outset
of the Oxford Movement that it would be interpreted
as a " Romanizing " Movement. By a curious cir-
cumstance, the spark which has been usually supposed
to have fired it—Keble's Assize Sermon[1]—was a protest against a legislative act that was part of a scheme
for assisting Roman Catholics which had the support of
the Government of the day. Catholic Emancipation

---

[1] Perhaps, however, too much importance has been ascribed
to this sermon. See my *Newman*, Appendix IV.

had directed attention to the disabilities under which the Irish Roman Catholics were then suffering; and legislative measures had been passed to bring about a relaxation of tithes formerly paid by Roman Catholics to the Established Church in Ireland. The plan to suppress a number of the superfluous Irish Bishoprics was part of the same scheme. The saving of revenue which it would effect was to recoup the Government for its loss of tithe revenue. When Keble attacked the Government in 1833, he was attacking them for giving relief to Roman Catholics. If Newman was right in dating the beginning of the Movement from July 14, 1833, then the Oxford Movement was begun explicitly to resist the progress of Romanism.

CHAPTER III

THE *Tracts for the Times* were begun in order to recall to men's minds the ancient heritage of the Church of England. This was clearly expressed in the Advertisement—dated November 1, 1834—which Newman prefixed to the first bound volume of them. The *Tracts*, he said, " were published with the object of contributing something towards the practical revival of doctrines which, although held by the great divines of our Church, at present have become obsolete with the majority of her members, and are withdrawn from public view even by the more learned and orthodox few who still adhere to them " (p. iii). The neglect of these doctrines had led " to a lamentable increase of sectarianism " (p. iii). " The awakened mind knows its wants, but cannot provide for them; and in its hunger will feed upon ashes, if it cannot obtain the pure milk of the word. Methodism and Popery are in different ways the refuge of those whom the Church stints of the gifts of grace; they are the foster-mothers of abandoned children " (p. iv). It is the belief of the contributors to the *Tracts*, so the Advertisement concluded, " that nothing but these neglected doctrines, faithfully preached, will repress that extension of Popery for which the ever multiplying divisions of the religious world are too clearly preparing the way " (p. v).

These passages make it clear that one of the primary objects of the *Tracts* was to resist the progress of Roman Catholicism. Another illustration of this is a printed *Memorandum for Friends*, circulated among those who were believed to be favourable to Tractarian principles.[1] In these printed instructions, friends of the Movement were asked to put the *Tracts* into the hands of their local bookseller, and " to provide him with a board, painted ' Tracts for the Times against Popery and Dissent,' and to see that it occupies a conspicuous place in his shop window." The Tractarian Movement, therefore, began as a protest against the claims of Rome.

The Tractarians, it is true, had good reasons for emphasizing their attitude to Romanism. From an early date the charge of " Popery " was laid at their feet. This charge was largely a conventional one, which had traditionally been applied by those of Low Church views to their opponents in the Establishment, and was not to be taken too seriously. It had long been the fashion to attribute " Popery " to those who held " High Church " views. In the Seventeenth Century it was an accusation constantly made against those of the Laudian school. There were no more grounds for supposing that Keble or Newman or Froude in 1833 would become Roman Catholics than for supposing that Andrewes or Jeremy Taylor or Hammond would have done so two centuries earlier. Nevertheless, the *Tract* writers must have anticipated from the outset that the charge of Romanizing would be made against them, and they had thus ample grounds for stressing their hostility to Popery. Accord-

---

[1] This document is reprinted in full in my *Newman*, Appendix II., pp. 159 *f.*, with additions in Newman's handwriting.

ingly, there is to be found in the early numbers of the *Tracts* a long series of passages in which the writers express in no measured terms their distrust of Romanist pretensions. Some of these we shall proceed to examine.

It is significant that the strongest of them come from the pen of Newman. Also, even allowing for the far greater number of *Tracts* that he wrote, they are much more frequent and forcible in his pages than in those of the other writers. One of the most vigorous of them occurs in *Tract No.* 20. Papists, he wrote, " act with great force upon the imaginations of men. The vaunted antiquity, the universality, the unanimity of their Church puts them above the varying fashions of the world and the religious novelties of the day. And truly when one surveys the grandeur of their system, a sigh arises in the thoughtful mind, to think that we should be separate from them. *Cum talis esses, utinam noster esses!* But, alas! AN UNION IS IMPOSSIBLE.[1] Their communion is infected with heterodoxy; we are bound to flee it, as a pestilence. They have established a lie in the place of God's truth; and by their claim of immutability in doctrine, cannot undo the sin they have committed. They cannot repent. Popery must be destroyed; it cannot be reformed " (No. 20, p. 3).

Again, God " has wonderfully preserved our Church as a true branch of the Church Universal, yet withal preserved it free from doctrinal error. It is Catholic and Apostolic, yet not Papistical. . . . Depend upon it, to insist on the doctrine of the Visible Church is not to favour the Papists, it is to do them the most serious

[1] Newman's capitals.

injury. It is to deprive them of their only strength "
(No. 20, pp. 3 f.). And again, " Rome has to confess
her Papal corruptions, and her cruelty towards those
who refuse to accept them " (No. 8, p. 4).

If the other early *Tract* writers were usually less
vigorous in their criticisms of Rome than Newman,
they were quite definite in their repudiation of her.
Thus Pusey wrote in his tract on the Eucharistic Sacrifice:
" The Romish Church corrupted and marred the
Apostolic doctrine in two ways—first, by the error of
Transubstantiation, secondly, by that of Purgatory;
and in both there occurs that peculiar corruption of
the administrators of the Romish Church, that they
countenance so much more of profitable [?] error than
in their abstract system they acknowledge " (No. 81,
p. 7).

And again, in one of his tracts on Baptism: " Alex-
andria, the bulwark of the faith in the Holy Trinity,
and North Africa, of the unmeritedness of God's free
grace, a desolation ! Rome, once characterized for
steady practical adherence to sound doctrine, a seat
of Anti-Christ. Geneva, once proposed as the model
for all reformed Churches, and of influence well-nigh
unbounded, and yet immediately the parent of Socin-
ianism, and now a prey to the heresy which came forth,
but was for the time ejected, also from its bosom !"
(No. 67, ed. 1836, p. 201).

Perceval wrote *Tract No.* 36 entitled "Account of
Religious Sects at Present Existing in England." In
it, the Sects are divided into three groups according
as they reject the truth altogether (*e.g.*, Jews); or receive
and teach a part, but not the whole of the truth (*e.g.*, the
Presbyterians); or teach more than the truth. In this

third category are named the Roman Catholics, the Swedenborgians, the Southcottians and the Irvingites. The first of these are " Romanists or Papists (so called because they are the followers of the Pope or Bishop of Rome) who teach that the images of God and of the Saints ought to be worshipped; that the Virgin Mary and other Saints ought to be prayed to; that in the Lord's Supper, after consecration, the bread is no longer bread, the wine no longer wine; that all Churches owe obedience to the Pope of Rome, etc. They have at different times attempted to confirm these doctrines by pretended miracles " (p. 5).

J. W. Bowden, Newman's intimate friend, in *Tract No.* 30, wrote thus: " We acknowledge the Pope and his Bishops in foreign countries to be, by station, ministers of the Church, though we admit and lament the fact that they have led the branches of it over which they preside into apostasy and shame; yet we feel that in sending their representatives hither, to act in defiance of the Church already established, they are exceeding the limits of their authority " (p. 6).

Tracts Nos. 27 and 28 are merely translations from John Cosin's treatise on Transubstantiation; yet they are issued with the original title unchanged—namely, " The History of Popish Transubstantiation; to which is opposed the Catholic Doctrine of the Holy Scripture, the Ancient Fathers, and the Reformed Churches."

The Tractarians from the outset laid great stress upon the necessity of the Apostolic Succession. This teaching by itself might appear to involve at least a pro-Roman tendency in the Movement. The Church of Rome, whatever her other failings, surely shared with us the possession of that episcopal succession which is essential for the Christian ministry. But, even in this matter of episcopal succession, the Tractarians drew a distinction between England and Rome. They believed, indeed, in a transmission of grace through the laying-on of hands. But they believed equally in the importance of a continuous succession through the historic sees; and accordingly did not naturally regard the Roman Catholic clergy in this country, who derived their Orders through the Vicars Apostolic, as Christian ministers in the true sense of the term. Accordingly, in his *Tract* on the Apostolical Succession (No. 4), Keble refers to the Church of England as being " the only Church in this realm which has a right to be quite sure that she has the Lord's body to give to His people " (p. 5).

The accusation of Popery against the *Tract* writers was apparently made within a year of the publication of the first *Tracts*. Thus, in " Via Media No. I." (No. 38), dated July 25, 1834, Newman had already to rebut the charge of Romanism. This *Tract* was written in dialogue form, and *Clericus* was defending the Tractarian position. " Men seem to think," said Clericus, " that we are plainly and indisputably proved to be Popish if we are proved to differ from the generality of Churchmen now-a-days " (p. 5). Yet Clericus would not allow the accusation. " In the Seventeenth Century," he replied, " the theology of the divines of the English Church was substantially the same as ours is; and it experienced the full hostility of the Papacy. It was the true *Via Media*; Rome sought to block up that way as fiercely as the Puritans " (p. 11). The *Via Media* thesis here propounded is further developed in Part II. of the *Tract* (*i.e.*, No. 41), which is dated

August 24 of the same year. "Our Church," Clericus argued here, "has taken the *Via Media* between [Protestantism] and Popery" (p. 6).

These are but a few of the anti-Roman passages contained in the *Tracts for the Times*. In the catena of anti-Papal extracts which Pusey published in 1839, over thirty of these extracts are taken from the *Tracts* themselves.

CHAPTER IV

THE FIRST CHARGES OF POPERY

IT was early in 1836 that the Tractarians made the sudden discovery that they were highly unpopular among a considerable section of the University, and a far larger section of the country as a whole. The circumstances connected with the expression of this feeling are as follows. On January 18, 1836, Edward Burton, the Regius Professor of Divinity, had died and shortly afterwards Dr. R. D. Hampden was announced as his successor. That the appointment should have aroused the suspicion and distrust of the Tractarians was only natural. Hampden was one of the leaders of the Liberal party, and had already become the object of widespread dislike through his open advocacy of the admission of Dissenters to the University. When, therefore, Hampden's appointment was published, the Tractarian leaders associated themselves with that wide body of feeling in the University which was opposed to it. They lent their support to measures which resulted in Hampden's being censured by a large majority of Convocation. This censure was widely criticized, more particularly outside Oxford; and in the circumstances the Tractarians had to bear the brunt of the criticism. Much more was ascribed to them in the matter than really belonged to them;

33   3

for the "conspiracy" against Hampden to which they had lent their support was the work of a far larger section of the University than those who held Tractarian views. The upshot of the incident was that the feeling against the Tractarians, which until that time had been more or less unorganized, suddenly burst into flame; and an active anti-Tractarian campaign began, which was to continue both in Oxford and elsewhere up till 1845, and long after.

A brilliant but vindictive article from the pen of Dr. Arnold attacked the "Oxford conspiracy" in the *Edinburgh Review* for April, 1836. It was entitled— though the title is said to have been the editor's and not Arnold's—"Dr. Hampden and the Oxford Malignants." He voiced the feeling of the rising opposition by his words: "Once only in the history of Christianity do we find a heresy—for never was that term more justly applied—so degraded and low-principled as this" (p. 235). But Arnold's brilliance was not by itself enough to sustain a campaign. It was necessary that some charge against the Tractarians should be found which would be popular and immediately understood; and the charge which was seized upon was that of "Popery."

In Oxford itself two literary productions began the attack. The former of them was entitled *A Pastoral Epistle from His Holiness the Pope to some Members of the University of Oxford, faithfully translated from the Original Latin*, and was written by one Dr. Charles Dickinson, who later became Bishop of Meath, and was a protégé of Whately's. The pamphlet was published in London in 1836. It was a shameless production, and, of its kind, not particularly clever. It certainly received greater attention than its merits demanded. In it the writers of the *Tracts* were grievously misrepresented. Thus the passage from Newman, *Tract No.* 20, p. 3, reproduced above,[1] was quoted, but curtailed at *noster esses*; in this way he was completely and purposely misrepresented. If the pamphlet had possessed real brilliance, such misrepresentations might have been atoned for. As it was, they were merely base.

Pusey, however, deemed that the *Pastoral* required a reply, and he published shortly afterwards *An Earnest Remonstrance to the Author of the Pope's Pastoral,* which was dated April 25, 1836. It was mainly a criticism of the method of the pamphlet, deploring the flippant treatment of such serious subjects. But Pusey insists also on the injustice of the imputation of " Popery " to the leaders. " You know," he remonstrates, " that these authors [*i.e.*, the Tractarians] had written also against Popery, and republished older writings against it; their very Tracts are known by the name of ' Tracts Against Popery and Dissent,' although, when they were commenced, Dissent was everywhere a pressing evil; Popery had scarcely begun to bestir itself, and was therefore the less noticed. You know that all occasions of guarding against the corruptions of Rome had been used in the very Tracts corrective of Dissent " (p. 32). To this passage there is the interesting footnote, " A new series of ' Tracts Against Romanism ' had meanwhile been actually commenced, although not then published." What ultimately became of these is not recorded.

The charge of Popery, once made, was never allowed to be forgotten. In the following year (1837) a pam-

[1] Cp. page 28.

phlet by Peter Maurice, a Chaplain of New College, saw the light with the title *The Popery of Oxford Confronted, Disavowed, and Repudiated.* This effusion was at least lively. Its author was almost a fanatic and smelt Popery everywhere, and a whole series of pamphlets against it issued from his pen. Before the Movement had begun, he had written a pamphlet with the title *Popery in Oxford,* to which reference has already been made in another context. In 1868 he is still declaiming against the " ritualism " of the churches of Oxford and the neighbourhood.[1] For the present-day reader, the chief interest of his pamphlet of 1837 rests in its allusions to the development of Tractarian ceremonial, a subject about which it is very difficult to obtain information. The " ritualism " to which Maurice objected was only of the simplest kind. He objected to the adoption of the Eastward position at St. Mary the Virgin's. He objected to the use of a credence table in Littlemore Church. He objected again to the use of a stole (apparently black) with a small St. Andrew's Cross at each end. He objected, it seems, to the minister kneeling on a cushion before the Communion table. He objected to the use of a reading desk. This was doubtless the extent of the ceremonial development at this early date, and presumably it was practically confined to the two churches within Newman's cure.

Similar attacks were directed against the Tractarians in the party journals and newspapers of the day. The *Christian Observer,* in attacking Pusey's Tract on Baptism, said that its author ought to lecture at Maynooth or the Vatican. It is evident from their context that the

[1] Among them St. Thomas, and St. Philip and St. James, Oxford; and the parish churches of Bloxham and Wantage.

charges of " Popery " were made, not because the Tractarians showed any likelihood of becoming Roman Catholics, but simply because they were reasserting the teaching of the " High Church " theologians of earlier times.

CHAPTER V

IN 1836 great interest was aroused by a course of lectures on the Roman Catholic Claims, delivered by Nicholas Wiseman at St. Mary's, Moorfields, in the Lent of that year. They attracted large crowds, and the audience was made up to a great extent of Protestants; among those who heard the future cardinal is said to have been the first Lord Brougham. They did not deal specifically with Anglicanism as expounded by the writers of the *Tracts*; but in view of the growing tendency to ascribe " Popery " to the Oxford leaders, it was essential that they on their part should produce some *apologia*.

Newman personally was far from disgusted at the shaking of Protestant prejudices which Wiseman's Lectures had occasioned. Writing in the *British Critic* for December, 1836—anonymously, of course—he said: " We hear with great equanimity the rumours of the impression which Dr. Wiseman's lectures have made upon the mixed multitude of London. Romanism has great truths in it which we of this day have almost forgotten, and its preachers will recall numbers of Churchmen and Dissenters to an acknowledgment of them." It is true that in the latter part of the article Newman proceeded to criticize with severity and acumen many of Wiseman's contentions; but those who were unaware of the subtleties of Newman's mind naturally regarded with suspicion his admission that Romanism contained great truths. The editor of the *British Critic* had his misgivings. S. F. Wood, an uncle of the present Lord Halifax, told Newman that the editor " was immensely disgusted with [his] Wiseman article, and declares that if another of the same kind is sent, he will throw up the editorship. They say you make Wiseman a peg to hang your attacks on Protestantism on."

The attention which Wiseman's Lectures directed to Romanism suggested the advisability of a treatise which should deal with the subject at length from the standpoint of the *Tracts*. A review article was far too limited a field for any adequate treatment of the problem. It was in these circumstances that Newman published his *Lectures on the Prophetical Office of the Church, viewed relatively to Romanism and Popular Protestantism*, in the early part of 1837. This set of Lectures was based on a correspondence which Newman had had in 1834 with a French Abbé, Jager, and the substance of them had been delivered in Adam de Brome's Chapel in St. Mary's, Oxford, in 1836.

In the collected edition of Newman's works, brought out long after he had become a Roman Catholic, this volume was reissued in *The Via Media of the Anglican Church*. This title, no less than the complete title of the original, was somewhat misleading; for though the *Via Media* hypothesis is referred to once or twice in them, the whole plan of the lectures is conceived with reference to the Roman issue; and, during Tractarian times, Newman constantly quoted them simply as

" *On Romanism.*" In point of fact they are a magnificent and far too little known *apologia* for Anglicanism as against the Roman claims. Newman wrote them when he was at the height of his powers, and they reflect the spirit of general optimism which at that date possessed the Tractarian leaders. Seldom has a controversial work been conducted on such a high *niveau*. From beginning to end it deals with the broad philosophical issues which separate the Anglican and Roman Catholic interpretations of religion, and the argument never degenerates into the discussion of trivialities.

At the outset Newman conceded that there were certain affinities which Rome had with Anglicanism but which had no corresponding place in Protestant dissent. Rome and Anglicanism both possessed the same fundamental faith; it was only the Roman corruptions which Anglicanism repudiated. But Newman insisted that a sharp contrast had to be drawn between Rome quiescent and Rome in action. " Viewed indeed in action, and as realized in its present partisans, it is but one of the many denominations which are the disgrace of our age and country " (p. 56). And, a little farther on, " Romanism, which even in its abstract system must be considered a perversion or distortion of the truth, is in its actual and public manifestation a far more serious error. It is then a disproportionate or monstrous development of a theory in itself extravagant " (p. 61).

The doctrine held by Roman Catholicism to which most attention is paid in these lectures is the doctrine of Infallibility. This is the subject of Lectures 3 and 4, which are entitled respectively " The Doctrine

of Infallibility Morally Considered " and " The Doctrine of Infallibility Politically Considered." The
whole temper of Romanism, with its over-definition
of dogmas, is rooted in the misguided belief that the
Church has the power to answer every problem in
heaven and earth. At bottom, in Newman's view,
religion is mysterious. " The human mind cannot
measure the things of the Spirit. Christianity is a
supernatural gift, originating in the unseen world and
only extending into this. It is a vast scheme, running
out into width and breadth, encompassing us round
about, not embraced by us " (p. 107). Accordingly,
" not the least pernicious peculiarity of Romanism "
is that " it professes to be a complete theology. It
arranges, adjusts, explains, exhausts, every part of the
Divine Economy. It may be said to leave no region
unexplored, no heights unattempted, rounding off its
doctrines with a neatness and finish which is destruc-
tive of many of the most noble and most salutary
exercises of mind in the individual Christian. That
feeling of awe and piety which the mysteriousness of
the Gospel should excite fades away under this fictitious
illumination which is poured over the entire Dis-
pensation. . . . Whether miracles have ceased, and,
if so, at what date ? How long Catholic doctrine was
preserved from human additions ? How far Gospel
privileges are extended to separatists ? How much
must be believed by individuals in order to salvation ?
What is the state of unbaptized infants ? What
amount of temporal punishment must be set against
the sins of accepted Christians ? What sort of change
takes place in the consecration of the Eucharist ? All
these are questions which man cannot determine, yet

such as these Romanists delight to handle " (pp. 108 *ff.*).
Arguments such as these make it clear that Newman
regarded the gulf which separates us from Rome to
consist not so much in specific dogmas as in the temper
which divides us. The difference is something far deeper
than any such problem as that of the relation of Popes
and General Councils. It is the difference between a
religion which is rooted in mystery and awe, and a
religion which is rooted in exact dogmatic definition.

Newman proceeded to express his opinion that this
temper of over-definition had resulted in grave moral
consequences. The Roman moral theologians treat
every action as though it were a piece of bargaining
with God. " Each deed has its price, every quarter
of the land of promise is laid down and described.
Roads are carefully marked out, and such as would
attain to perfection are constrained to move in certain
lines, as if there were a science of gaining heaven "
(p. 123). In consequence, " a secondary standard of
holiness " has been laid down as adequate for the
ordinary Christian. The standard of morality which
is sought by the saint need not be attempted by the
Christian who wishes merely to save his soul. Whole-
hearted devotion to God is not expected of the average
believer. " If, indeed, there is one offence more than
the rest characteristic of Romanism, it is this, its in-
dulging the carnal tastes of the multitude of men,
setting a limit to their necessary obedience, and ab-
solving them from the duty of sacrificing their whole
lives to God. And this serious deceit is in no small
degree the necessary consequence of that completeness
and minuteness in its theology to which the doctrine
of Infallibility gives rise " (p. 124).

Rome, again, is distrustful of Antiquity, and this distrust is another corollary of the same temper. " Our [Foundation] is Antiquity; theirs the existing Church " (p. 85). The Romanist prefers syllogisms to history, " abstract proof to argument from fact. Facts, indeed, are confessedly troublesome, and must be avoided as much as possible by anyone who is bound by his theory to decide as well as dispute, much more if he professes himself infallible. . . . To appeal to facts is to put the controversy out of their own hands, and to lodge the decision with the world at large " (p. 132). Newman then proceeded to argue that the whole Roman doctrine of the Treasury of Merit was based on abstract reasoning. The Romanist " does not even attempt to detect his doctrine in the writings of the Fathers " (p. 137).

Throughout these lectures, many hard things are said about the Church of Rome. " She is a Church beside herself, abounding in noble gifts and rightful titles, but unable to use them religiously; crafty, obstinate, wilful, malicious, cruel, unnatural, as mad-men are. Or rather, she may be said to resemble a demoniac; possessed with principles, thoughts, and tendencies not her own, in outward form and in out-ward powers what God made her, but ruled within by an inexorable spirit, who is sovereign in his manage-ment over her, and most subtle and most successful in the use of her gifts. . . . I must not be supposed to deny that there is any real excellence in Romanism even as it is, or any really excellent men adherents to it. Satan ever acts on a system. . . . In Romanism there are some things absolutely good, some things only just tainted and sullied, some things corrupted, and some things in themselves sinful; but the system itself so called, as a whole, and therefore all parts of it, tend to evil " (p. 102). Rome is among the false prophets who are to be discerned by their fruits. Among the marks which betray her are " her denying the cup to the laity, her idolatrous worship of the Blessed Virgin, her Image-worship, her recklessness in anathematizing, and her schismatical and overbearing spirit " (p. 317).

CHAPTER VI

HURRELL FROUDE had died on February 28, 1836. A man of exceptional ability and deep piety, he had been one of the most enthusiastic of those who supported Tractarian principles. Yet his friends felt how little the tangible fruit of his short life corresponded with his talents. Cut off from active participation in the course of the Movement from 1833 onwards, Froude had left behind him only an inconsiderable legacy of published works. Newman and Keble accordingly decided to edit and publish a collection of his *Remains*, derived partly from his private diaries, partly from his letters, partly from his sermons, and partly from his papers. The first two volumes to appear came out early in the year 1838.

Their publication created a storm. Froude had been fearless in conversation and had constantly held up to ridicule the Englishman's conventional prejudices. He hated pretence and hypocrisy of every kind. Hugh James Rose used to say of him that he was " not afraid of inferences." He had a passion for Medievalism; and he had no hesitation in expressing his admiration of Medieval saints and his hatred of the Reformers. His editors were determined to proceed with their task in the spirit of Froude's own sincerity. Nothing of importance should be withheld. Froude should be presented to the public just as he was, and his unconventionality should be a challenge to the world to lay aside cant and shams. Froude was to be shown to have been ruthlessly critical—but if ruthlessly critical of others, no less ruthlessly critical of himself.

Froude's attitude to Rome must be understood through the sharp contrast which he drew between Rome as she was in ideal and Rome as she was in actual fact. He sympathised with Rome as an ideal. But he had little affection for Rome as an existing institution. He had travelled abroad with Newman in the winter of 1832-1833, and what he had then seen of the Church of Rome had shocked him even more than it had Newman. Speaking of Italy and Sicily, he said: "These Catholic countries seem in an especial manner κατέχειν τὴν ἀλήθειαν ἐν ἀδικίᾳ; and the priesthood are themselves so sensible of the hollow basis on which their power rests, that they dare not resist the most atrocious encroachments of the state upon their privileges. . . . I have seen priests laughing when at the Confessional; and indeed it is plain, that unless they habitually made light of very gross immorality, three-fourths of the population [of Naples] would be excommunicated" (i. 293 f.).

The Council of Trent came in for particular condemnation at the hands of Froude. He seems to have regarded this as having corrupted the much purer Church of Medieval times. At an interview which he and Newman had with Wiseman at Rome in the spring of 1833, they learnt that Rome would receive no converts " without swallowing the Council of Trent as a whole " (i. 307). After describing the interview further, Froude recorded in his jesting way: " —— [doubtless Newman] declares that ever since I heard this,

I have become a staunch Protestant, which is a most base calumny on his part, though I own it has altogether changed my notions of the Roman Catholics and made me wish for the total overthrow of their system. I think that the only τόπος now is ' the ancient Church of England,' and as an explanation of what one means, ' Charles the First and the Nonjurors ' " (pp. 307 f.).

The passages in the *Remains* which aroused most hostility were those in which Froude condemned without qualification the Reformers. This was the counterpart of his condemnation of the Tridentine Bishops. Both corrupted the purer teaching of Medieval times. Readers of a hundred years ago were scandalized when they heard Cranmer and his allies held up to obloquy. " As to the Reformers," he wrote, " I think worse and worse of them. Jewell was what you would in these days call an irreverent dissenter. His Defence of his Apology disgusted me more than almost any work I have read. Bishop Hickes and Dr. Brett I see go all lengths with me in this respect, and I believe Laud did. The Preface to the Thirty-nine Articles was certainly intended to disconnect us from the Reformers " (pp. 379 f.). And again: " Really I hate the Reformation and the Reformers more and more, and have almost made up my mind that the rationalist spirit they set afloat is the ψευδοπροφήτης of the Revelations " (p. 389). And still more definitely: " Also why do you praise Ridley ? Do you know sufficient good about him to counterbalance the fact that he was the associate of Cranmer, Peter Martyr, and Bucer? N.B.—How beautifully the *Edinburgh Review* has shown up Luther, Melanchthon, and Co. ! What genius has possessed them to do our dirty work? . . . *Pour moi*, I never mean, if I can help it, to use any phrases even, which can connect me with such a set. I shall never call the Holy Eucharist ' the Lord's Supper,' nor God's priests ' ministers of the Word,' or the Altar ' the Lord's table,' etc., etc.; innocent as such phrases are in themselves, they have been dirtied; a fact of which you seem oblivious on many occasions. Nor shall I even abuse the Roman Catholics *as a church* for anything except excommunicating us " (pp. 393 *ff.*).

It must be noticed that Froude's feelings with respect to Rome differed widely from time to time, depending largely on circumstances. Thus in a letter written from Naples in 1833 he wrote: " Since I have been out here I have got a worse notion of the Roman Catholics than I had. I really do think them idolaters, though I cannot be quite confident of my information as it affects the character of the priests. . . . What I mean by calling these people idolaters is, that I believe they look upon the Saints and Virgin as good-natured people that will try to get them let off easier than the Bible declares, and that, as they don't intend to comply with the conditions on which God promises to answer prayers, they pray to them as a come-off. But this is a generalization for which I have not sufficient data " (I. xiii *f.*). As opposed to this, a passage written about a year later from Barbados runs: " You will be shocked at my avowal that I am every day becoming a less and less loyal son of the Reformation. It appears to me plain that in all matters that seem to us indifferent or even doubtful, we should conform our practices to those of the Church which has preserved its traditionary practices unbroken. We cannot know about any seemingly indifferent practice of the Church of Rome that it is not a development of the apostolic ἦθος; and it is to no purpose to say that we can find no proof of it in the writings of the six first centuries; they must find a *dis*proof if they would do anything " (p. 336). With both these passages should be compared the remark: The Romanists [are not schismatics in England and Catholics abroad, but they] " are wretched Tridentines everywhere " (i. 434).

The third and fourth volumes of the *Remains* appeared a year later, in 1839. These volumes are introduced by a long Preface, written, it is said, by Keble, though both the editors accepted the responsibility for it. In it, reference is made to the stir which the preceding volumes had evoked; this, the editors observed somewhat sardonically, at least implied that the teaching in them was such as had relation to the present age. But they went on to identify themselves with the main tenor of Froude's characteristic views. They spoke of " that, which more than anything else in these *Remains* [*i.e.*, in vols. i. and ii.], seems to have startled and displeased many who in principle would agree with the writer, [namely] the unfavourable mention made from time to time of the Reformers as a party; and inclusively of the English Reformers." They added: " Undoubtedly it appeared to him—and his editors, by publishing his sentiments on that head so unreservedly, without any kind of disavowal, intimated of course their own general acquiescence in the opinion —that the persons chiefly instrumental in that great change were not, as a party, to be trusted on ecclesiastical and theological questions " (p. xix). And later, " It cannot be too carefully inculcated . . . that the

4

cause of the English Church is not at all mixed up, neither in reason nor in fact, with the personal conduct or theological opinions of her Reformers " (p. xxii). The contents of these two later volumes have little bearing on the subject of these chapters, however; the second is an account of the struggle between Henry II. and " Thomas à Becket " (the form used by Froude).

A passage in a letter to Perceval, written from Barbados on September 9, 1834, sums up Froude's position. In it he wrote: " If I was to assign my reason for belonging to the Church of England in preference to any other religious community, it would be simply this, that she has retained an apostolical clergy, and enacts no sinful terms of communion; whereas, on the one hand, the Romanists, though retaining an apostolical clergy, do exact sinful terms of communion; and on the other, no other religious community has retained such a clergy " (Perceval, *Collection*, p. 16).   Froude had little knowledge of the technicalities of the Roman controversy.   But he fully realized that the popular hostility to Rome, no less than the popular adulation of the Reformers, was nine-tenths prejudice; and these prejudices he was glad to expose.   He had an affection for those elements in Rome which had survived from the Middle Ages, as is shown, *e.g.*, by his use of the Breviary.   But this affection is an indication of his " Medievalism," not of his " Romanism." There is no language about Rome's being " the centre of unity " such as was to be found in the writings of the Romanizing party a few years later.

CHAPTER VII

THE EFFECT OF FROUDE'S "REMAINS"

THE sporadic charges of Popery which had been made against the leaders of the Movement up to 1838 became a veritable onslaught with the publication of the first two volumes of Froude's *Remains*. These volumes produced first a shudder of horror and then a howl of rage. Shortly after they had appeared, Lord Morpeth denounced the Tractarians in the House of Lords as " a sect of damnable and detestable heretics of late sprung up in Oxford, a sect which evidently affects popery and merits the heartiest condemnation of all true Christians." In Oxford, the attack was begun in earnest by the Lady Margaret Professor of Divinity, Dr. Godfrey Faussett, who preached to the University on May 20, 1838, a sermon on " the Revival of Popery." This sermon was published a little later. In it, it is true, Faussett concerned himself not only with the Tractarians, but also with the rapid spread of Roman Catholicism which had taken place since the Emancipation Act. But the Tractarians came in for the full force of his attack. " To affirm that these persons are strictly Papists, or that within certain limits of their own devising they are not actually opposed to the corruptions and the Communion of Rome, would," he admitted, " be as uncharitable as it is untrue.

But," he went on to ask, " who shall venture to pronounce them safe and consistent members of the Church of England ? And who shall question the obvious tendency of their views to Popery itself?" (p. 24). Froude's *Remains*, in particular, came in for the Margaret Professor's severest censures.

The news reached Newman that Faussett intended to publish his sermon, and he set himself to reply. With his amazing powers of composition, he was able to send to the printer the text of a hundred-page pamphlet on the day after Faussett's sermon had issued from the press. The circumstances demanded that the *Letter to the Rev. Godfrey Faussett* should deal chiefly with Froude's *Remains*, which had especially come in for the Professor's attack. The line that Newman took was that, even if some of Froude's teaching were not the official teaching of the English Church, the English Church had always allowed her members a latitude of opinion which was not confined by her promulgated formularies; and as an instance of this he quoted a number of passages from Bramhall which went uncondemned in the Seventeenth Century. In an eloquent passage at the end of the *Letter*, Newman insisted that " the way to withstand and repel the Romanists " was " not by cries of alarm, and rumours of plots, and dispute, and denunciation, but by living up to the creeds, the services, the ordinances, the usages of our own Church without fear of consequences, without fear of being called Papists; to let matters take their course freely, and to trust to God's good Providence for the issue " (p. 98).

The increasing prominence into which attacks such as that of Faussett brought the Tractarians led the

Bishop of Oxford, Bagot, to allude with some misgivings to the writers of the *Tracts* in his charge in
the summer of 1838. It is true that his criticism was
only very lenient. But the press, ever ready at this
juncture to decry the Tractarians, made the most of it.
Bagot pointed out that he himself was constantly asked
to take action against the leaders of the Movement.
He had, he said, been " continually (though anonymously) appealed to in [his] official capacity to check
breaches both of doctrine and discipline, through the
growth of Popery among us " (p. 19). On the score
of discipline Bagot fully exonerated the Tractarians,
but he added that, while he believed much of their
teaching valuable in the face of liberalism, he had
apprehensions as to the effect which some of their
doctrines might produce, particularly on their disciples;
and he implored them " by the purity of their intentions,
to be cautious, both in their writings and actions, to
take heed lest their good be evil spoken of; lest in their
exertions to re-establish unity, they unhappily create
fresh schism; lest in their admiration of antiquity, they
revert to practices which heretofore have ended in
superstition " (p. 21). The censure here implied, if
such it can be called, was of the mildest. Nevertheless,
as Newman wrote at the time, " a Bishop's lightest
word *ex cathedra* is heavy. His judgment on a book
cannot be light. It is a rare occurrence." It was a
sign of the growing fears of Popery.

The avowedly Low Church party exercised no such
restraint in their attacks on the Movement. *Letters
on the Writings of the Fathers*, by the anonymous Misopapisticus, was a work published in 1838 by the Low
Church publisher Seeley. It was composed mainly

of letters which had previously appeared in the *Record* newspaper. " The abettors of this system," wrote Misopapisticus, " are entirely alien to our Church, being the legitimate sons of the Romish communion " (p. 181). The whole tendency of the *Tracts for the Times* is towards Anti-Christ. " Increase rituals after the fashion of the Church of Rome, make them very important things, enhance the value of Sacraments, exalt the visible Church, represent it as the only medium of communication between God and His people, and depreciate faith in Christ and individual communion with God, and you will not fail to produce the awful apostasy which Irenæus describes, the very apostasy of Anti-Christ; and this is the manifest tendency of the doctrines of the Oxford Tracts. Let all therefore beware of them who dread this enormous sin. The spirit of apostate Rome is evidently working at Oxford with all its accustomed subtleness and plausibility " (p. 250). From 1838 onwards, attacks such as this were part of the order of the day.

Hitherto the replies to the charge of Popery had been made with light weapons. Early in 1839, a new stage in the conflict was reached when Pusey directed his heavy guns against the enemy. The stimulus which led Pusey to undertake this work seems to have come ultimately from the Archbishop of Canterbury; for the Archbishop (Howley) had written to Bagot on the subject of Froude's *Remains*, and the Archbishop's opinion was passed on by Bagot to Pusey. " The prejudice against the editors," wrote the Archbishop, " is very rapidly spreading, and I fear will deprive the world of a great part of the benefit which it might otherwise derive from their talents, learning, and industry, applied to the elucidation of religious truth and eccesiastical history. In justice to themselves and the public, I think they would do well to take some opportunity of showing to the world that they are not hostile to the Reformation. I entirely acquit them of the charge, but many respectable persons will pronounce them guilty " (Liddon's *Life of Pusey*, ii. 72). Pusey accordingly set to work to defend himself and his friends against the imputation of Popery. His defence took the form of a Letter addressed to the Bishop of Oxford, the text alone of which ran to nearly 240 pages. It was published about the end of March, 1839, and bore the title *On the Tendency to Romanism imputed to Doctrines held of Old and Now, in the English Church.*

The Letter contains a clear statement of the grounds on which Pusey rejected the Roman claims. They are rooted in Rome's exclusiveness. The promised indefectibility of the Universal Church is used by Rome as a device to further her own purpose. It is " to become the safeguard of the one see of Rome, and to draw all other Churches to her footstool. This has been the πρῶτον ψεῦδος of Romanism, and her imposture, that she has claimed to herself the promise, which belonged to the whole Church. A high dignity belonged to her as the Apostolic Church of the West, and her traditions, as long as she kept them faithfully, had, naturally, a great estimation, when testimony was to be borne to Catholic truth; but she, instead of being ' among the first three,' would be alone, would have her voice not only essential, but alone essential; would make at all events the infallibility of a Council to depend upon the confirmation of her bishop; teaching oftentimes also that even particular Councils approved by the Pope became infallible, or that a general Council, in itself fallible, acquired an *ex post facto* infallibility through his approval. And thus like him who was high among ' the sons of God,' but would be higher than his Creator made him, she fell " (pp. 45 *ff*.).

In a significant passage on pp. 135 *f*. Pusey strongly criticized Rome for abandoning Communion in both kinds. He referred to the refusal of the cup to the laity as " *one* of the practical grievances of the Church of Rome, which should alone, without further disputing, restrain any from joining himself to her Communion. How it may be with those who have access to no other, we have no right to determine, though one cannot doubt but that they sustain herein a grievous loss; and the miserable state of Roman Catholic countries in general may be, in part, owing to this loss. But for any voluntarily to cast himself out of a Communion as our own, in the which he may receive it, and to join himself to that in which it is denied him, is such wanton trifling with privileges and casting away of God's gifts, and tempting of Him, that I should think this ground alone (which any plain man can understand) reason enough why no member of our Church should join her."

Pusey summed up by maintaining that so far from Tractarianism being a pro-Roman Movement, the influence of its teachings had hitherto been mainly " in the contrary and their rightful direction, furnishing a resting-place from Romanism to some who were wandering thither, and recovering others from it to the bosom of our English branch of the Church " (p. 238). If Romanists, he says, occasionally pay compliments to the Tractarians, and are sincere in so doing, then this is because they believe that Romanism is to be found in Antiquity, and they realise that the Anglican system wishes to be a faithful representative of Antiquity (p. 223).

Appended to this Letter was a catena[1] of extracts from Tractarian publications, "showing that to oppose Ultra-Protestantism is not to favour Popery." This was the most impressive part of the pamphlet. There are 101 passages in all taken from the *Tracts* themselves, from the *Lyra Apostolica*, and from the writings of Pusey, Newman, Froude and Keble. The captions in the index to this catena are indicative of the consistently critical attitude of the Tractarians towards Romanism. Thus, under the heading "*Popery*" there are the sub-headings: "incurable," "a falling off," "pestilential," "malicious and cruel," "rebellious," "tyrannical," "an insanity," "an evil spirit," "heretical," "exclusive," "irreconcilably different from us," "unscriptural," "presumptuous," "persecuting," "political," "rationalizes," "an Anti-Christ."

---

[1] This catena is not easy of access, but it is much the most important single document bearing on the subject of these pages, and deserves very careful study. It may be added here (though the present investigation does not carry the story beyond 1845) that the same anti-Roman witness is to be found in the writings of J. M. Neale and H. P. Liddon. In February, 1843, in a letter published in the press, Newman withdrew his fiercer polemical assertions against Rome. The substance of this letter, with additions, is to be seen in the preface to the *Essay on Development*, dated October 6, 1845.

CHAPTER VIII

A HIGHLY important stage in the history of the Anglo-Catholic revival was reached in the year 1838. It was heralded by a number of young Oxford men, chief of whom were Frederick Oakeley and William George Ward, both Fellows of Balliol College, joining the Movement. Of similar views were C. Seager, J. B. Morris, F. W. Faber, and J. D. Dalgairns. These men possessed widely different ideals from those of the original leaders. Newman described their position in the *Apologia* (ed. 1931, p. 259), where he wrote: " A new school of thought was rising, as is usual in such movements, and was sweeping the original party of the movement aside, and was taking its place. The most prominent person in it was a man of elegant genius, of classical mind, of rare talent in literary composition—Mr. Oakeley. . . . He had entered late into the Movement; he did not know its first years; and, beginning with a new start, he was naturally thrown together with that body of eager, acute, resolute minds who had begun their Catholic life about the same time as he, who knew nothing about the *Via Media* but had heard much about Rome." Dean Church wrote with reference to them: " The tendency of this section of able men was unquestionably Romewards, almost from the beginning of their connexion with the Movement" (p. 208). Accordingly, they may best be described as the Romanizing party.

In Oxford—Oakeley left Oxford in 1839—much the most influential figure in this group was William George Ward. One of the most brilliant dialecticians in the University, he combined with exceptional intellectual acumen the deepest moral earnestness. For history, it is true, he had but little regard. He knew little about it, and saw no reason to wish to know more; and any appeal to history left him quite unmoved. That Ward was more partial to Rome than the original leaders is therefore easily explicable; for the appeal to the Fathers has always been one of the chief weapons in the Anglican claim as against Rome from the days of Jewel onwards, and the Tractarians in particular recognized the force of the appeal to Antiquity. But to Ward the question whether modern Anglicanism or modern Romanism best represented the Church of Antiquity was a matter of minor importance. What he was concerned with was which interpretation of Christianity was most defensible as a living system.

Moreover, temperamentally Ward had for long been attracted to some parts of the Roman Catholic system. His unhistorical mind led him to attach but little importance to English religious tradition. He felt, and did not hesitate to avow, a dislike of prayers in set forms of words. "The Anglican communion service, beautiful as he found its prayers, *oppressed* him from the obligation it involved of his following at another's pace and in another's train of thought."[1] Ward used

[1] W. Ward, *William George Ward and the Oxford Movement*, p. 93.

to frequent the Roman Catholic chapel in Spanish Place, London, long before he joined the Tractarians; and thus brought to the Tractarian Movement sympathies of a definitely Roman Catholic type.

It was this group of theologians which was mainly responsible for inaugurating the ceremonial revival at Oxford. It initiated changes, the development of which were to figure largely in the subsequent history of Anglo-Catholicism; but at this date such questions were of relatively little significance. Far more important than any ceremonial approximations to Rome were the doctrinal approximations of the Romanizing group; and to the consideration of these we must now turn.

The *British Critic* became increasingly the organ of this group. It was a quarterly theological publication which had been begun, in its then current series, in 1827. Newman became editor of it in July, 1838, and continued as such until 1841; and during these years its pages were largely filled with the contributions of the Romanizing party. From the beginning of his editorship of it, Newman had granted his contributors a considerable degree of freedom, and allowed articles to appear with which he himself disagreed. In 1841, when the *Tract No.* 90 affair led him to withdraw as far as possible from his leadership of the Movement, the editorship of the *British Critic* passed into the hands of Thomas Mozley of Oriel. All the articles appeared anonymously, though the names of the contributors were widely known in Oxford.

The group which centred in Ward and Oakeley made no attempt to conceal their Romanizing sympathies; and the English Roman Catholics were not slow in responding. Monsignor Wiseman, who now professed sanguine hopes of winning converts from the Tractarians to Roman Catholicism, began a series of articles in the *Dublin Review* on the subject of Anglicanism; and these articles, which were eagerly read by the pro-Roman group, produced a profound effect. Palmer (*Narrative of Events*, pp. 69 *f.*) says that already in 1839 there were in Oxford considerable doubts as to the validity of Anglican Orders as a result of one of these articles. The attack here referred to was sufficiently strong to lead Palmer to publish a reply which bore the title *The Apostolical Jurisdiction of the Episcopacy in the British Churches, vindicated against the Objections of Dr. Wiseman in the " Dublin Review."* It became fairly clear to those inside the Movement from about 1840 onwards that there was a real danger of secession, and from 1841 this danger was openly admitted. Thus Newman, in his *Letter to Jelf* on the occasion of *Tract No.* 90, said that the object of the *Tract* had been to keep certain individuals—obviously meaning Ward and his friends—from " straggling in the direction of Rome "; while Pusey, in *The Articles Treated of in Tract* 90 *Reconsidered*, spoke of " the acknowledged tendency of certain individuals in our Church to Romanism."

The " Romanism " of this group may be said to have consisted chiefly in four things. These were: (1) A willingness to accord a definite supremacy to the Roman See; (2) a distrust of the Reformation; (3) a belief in the possibility of corporate reunion with Rome; and (4) a love for Roman Catholic ceremonial forms. The fourth of these became an important influence on certain minds and it will be treated in the next chapter. But something must be said here of the remaining three.

In his *Narrative of Events*, published in 1843, Palmer not unjustly described the attitude of this group towards Rome as follows. Among them, he said, remarks were sometimes heard " indicating a disposition to acknowledge the supremacy of the See of Rome, to give way to *all its claims* however extreme, to represent it as the conservative principle of religion and society in various ages; and in the same spirit, those who are in any way opposed to the highest pitch of Roman usurpations are sometimes looked on as little better than heretics. The Gallican and the Greek Churches are considered unsound in their opposition to the claims of Rome. The latter is held to be separated from *Catholic* unity. The ' See of St. Peter ' is described as the centre of that unity; while our state of separation from it is regarded, not merely as an evil, but a sin—a cause of deep humiliation, a *judgment for our sins* ! The blame of separation, of schism, is openly and unscrupulously laid on the English Church ! . . . Displeasure is felt and expressed if any attempts are made to expose the errors, corruptions, and idolatries approved in the Roman communion " (pp. 149 *f.*).

An instance of such teaching from one of the Romanizing group itself is to be found in Dodsworth's printed letter to Sibthorp.[1] R. W. Sibthorp, sometime Fellow of Magdalen, had seceded to Rome in 1841, and W. Dodsworth issued his letter in 1842 under the title *Why have you Become a Roman Catholic?* On page 12 of this letter Dodsworth wrote: " Let us clearly understand wherein we agree and wherein we differ. We

[1] This clergyman, in Gladstone's words, " thrice cleared the chasm which separates the Church of England from the Church of Rome." See the article on " Sibthorp " in Ollard's *Dict. Eng. Ch. Hist.*

agree in desiring to see the Christian world united. We, with you, wish to have communion with the See of Rome, if Rome were other than she now is. And though we demur to the claim of the Pope's supremacy in the sense which the Romanists contend for it, we do not object to the idea so much insisted upon by you, that, in a united Church, the occupant of St. Peter's chair would be a symbol of the Church's centre of unity. But we differ upon the point which you so quietly assume—viz., that the Church of Rome is the same in almost every minute particular which it had been in the sixth century." And further on in the letter he wrote: " Nor do we need you to teach us that the younger Church of England should regard with reverence the elder and apostolically founded Church of Rome, and acknowledge the centre of unity for the Christian world to be in Rome, and not in Canterbury " (p. 18). But, he went on: " We appreciate, we trust, the value of unity. Let Catholic terms of unity be proposed to us, and we will gladly embrace them if you can show that we have not already embraced them. We are willing to confess, and do confess, that a large measure of the blame of disunion lies upon us; but we dare not add sin to sin by seeking union at the expense of TRUTH. All things short of this we ought to sacrifice for such an object. This we can NEVER sacrifice; and so we commit our cause to God " (pp. 18 f.).

That this desire for corporate reunion with Rome was widespread among the Romanizers at the time of *Tract No.* 90 is attested also by Oakeley in his *History of the Tractarian Movement* (p. 55).

The nemesis of the Romanizing teaching of this group was reached by Ward's famous *Ideal of a Christian*

Church (1844), wherein he defended the thesis that it was possible, nay that it was right, for English Churchmen to hold the whole *corpus* of official Roman Catholic doctrine. The ground on which he defended this paradoxical position was somewhat as follows:

' If the English Church is to be revived so as to fulfil her Divine mission, it is essential that she should have some ideal to which to approximate herself. Now the one branch of the Catholic Church which in any sense presents that ideal is the Church of Rome. She has corruptions in her borders, it is true. These must be discovered, and when discovered be removed from the concept of the *ideal*. But the fact remains that " Rome has preserved in the main, and we have not, what is so inestimably precious, the high and true *idea* of a Church; that whatever may be the present lukewarmness of her children—of which " (adds Ward) " for myself I really cannot judge nor have ever expressed an opinion—whenever zeal, energy, and piety revive, they can act immediately on the Church by *means* of the system they find, while among us they must begin by *attacking* the system they find " ' (pp. 53 *f.*).

Ward denied that such an attitude implied any lack of affection for the English Church. He paralleled the case of an American subject, who preferred the state of affairs before the revolt, and did all in his power to restore constitutional monarchy in America for what he believed to be the good of his country; such a one, he said, could not be accused of lack of patriotism (p. 54). The fact remains that, however great Ward's protestations of affection for the Church of England, he left it for Rome the year after he published the *Ideal*.

CHAPTER IX

THE CEREMONIAL REVIVAL

ONE aspect of Tractarianism which had considerable influence in connexion with the Romeward tendencies of the Movement, real and merely alleged, was the ceremonial revival to which it led. The earliest Tractarians had singularly little interest in ceremonial. But gradually, from about 1837 onwards, attempts were made by some of the followers of the Movement to reintroduce into the English Church ancient religious ceremonies and customs. As Canon Ollard has brought out in his *Short History of the Oxford Movement* (pp. 159 *ff.*), the most influential figure in this part of the revival was Dr. John Rouse Bloxam, who returned to Oxford to reside as Fellow of Magdalen in 1836. Bloxam had few claims as a theologian; but he was a learned antiquary and liturgiologist, and had been much influenced by Palmer's *Origines Liturgicæ* (1832). In 1837 Newman appointed him as his curate to serve at Littlemore, and this charge he held until 1840. Here, in the new church which was dedicated in 1836, he had scope for giving expression to his ceremonial interests. The altar had two candlesticks of gilded wood; there were two standard candlesticks in the sanctuary; there was also a wooden alms dish. Further—and, in the eyes of most English Churchmen of the time, far worse—Dr. Bloxam used to wear a (black?) silk stole. The opposition which these innovations occasioned may be discovered from the description of them in Peter Maurice's *The Popery of Oxford*, already alluded to.

Bloxam's innovations were the prototype of many more. Once the idea of ceremonial development had been suggested, there were few limits to its possibilities. The Prayer Book clearly allowed for a much fuller ceremonial than was to be found anywhere in the English Church at the beginning of the last century. A revival in ceremonial was, indeed, the natural counterpart of the reviving devotional life. Regular and systematic habits of prayer, emphasis upon the keeping of Saints' days, fasting as a means to holiness, brought with them in their train the need for fuller external expression.

If the majority of the original Tractarians stood somewhat aloof from the ceremonial revival at its outset, the Romanizing party warmly welcomed it. As has been already mentioned, Ward had for long been attracted to Roman Catholic worship which he attended in the vacations in London. Those who looked to Rome for their theology could hardly be expected to be uninfluenced by Roman forms of worship. Roman Catholic devotional books began to be used by the Oxford leaders of this group, and the practice of saying the " Hours " spread. In this way, the demand for a ceremonial revival became general among the Romanizing party.

From 1839 onwards the centre of this revival was the Margaret Chapel—a building on the present site of All Saints', Margaret Street. Structurally it was a singularly ill-adapted building for the purpose; an account of the obstacles which had to be contended with will be found in Oakeley's *History of the Tractarian Movement*. Oakeley became priest-in-charge here in 1839, and copied the altar ornaments from those in use at Littlemore. Judged by present-day standards, the ceremonial of this chapel was of the simplest. Nevertheless, it was far more elaborate than that of the churches of the original Tractarians. Ward was regularly consulted by Oakeley on any proposed innovations, and this chapel became the natural place of worship in London for those who held the less anti-Roman doctrines of the Ward group.

An instance of the suspicions which any ceremonial contact with Rome aroused at that date may be seen by the following incident, termed by Newman (when its significance had been long forgotten) the " Bloxam Escapade." In 1839 Bloxam paid a visit to Dr. Rock, the learned antiquarian, and during it attended Mass in the Roman Catholic chapel at Lord Shrewsbury's house.[1] A rumour got abroad that Bloxam had actually worshipped the Host. When charged with this offence —for so Newman judged it—Bloxam replied that he had merely been in the habit of frequenting the church in order to say his Office, that on one occasion there happened to be a Mass going on at the time at which he said Morning Prayer, and that during it he had continued to remain kneeling as he had done on other days. Nevertheless the incident produced some consternation, and Newman thought the matter of such importance that he informed his Bishop (Bagot) of what his curate had done.

[1] This was at Alton Towers, where Dr. Rock was then chaplain to Lord Shrewsbury.

From Bloxam's practice, the use of the stole was adopted at an early date by William Palmer, of Magdalen College, and also by Charles Seager, who introduced it into St. Thomas's Church, Oxford. Subsequently both of these clergymen, as well as many of the congregation of the Margaret Chapel, became Roman Catholics. There can be little doubt that in its earlier stages the ceremonial revival stimulated longings for the richer ritual of Rome. It was only as the century advanced that these desires were fully met by such churches as St. Barnabas', Pimlico, and All Saints', Margaret Street in London.

CHAPTER X

THE TRACTARIANS AND THE ROMANIZERS

THE rapid growth from 1838 onwards of opinions such as those held by Ward and Oakeley did not leave the original Tractarians unmoved. It was manifest that what the Romanizers were proclaiming as Anglo-Catholicism was a very different account of Anglicanism from that advocated in 1833. In the circumstances of the time, the position of the original leaders was an exceedingly difficult one. At the moment when opposition to Tractarian teaching was becoming greater every day, they had no wish to emphasize dissensions within their own ranks, nor to disown those who claimed to be their zealous supporters. Not unnaturally, the attitude taken up towards the new disciples varied greatly. Palmer of Worcester College had no sympathy whatever with the new school, and in 1843 wrote his *Narrative of Events* with the purpose of showing that the teaching of the Romanizers was poles removed from that with which he and his friends were concerned in 1833 and 1834. Pusey, though not realizing the danger of secession, himself disliked the teaching of the group. His policy at the time was to prevent an open rupture, perhaps in the hope that affairs would in due course better themselves. Newman, who was far more intimately associated with the new group than the others, and, with his pliable nature, more influenced by it, knew that secession was a real danger. He certainly could not have been induced to embark on a campaign against them. It was in his dealings with this group that he precipitated the crisis of 1841.

For over twelve months before *Tract No.* 90 was written Newman had been aware of the possibility of secession taking place. In the summer of 1839 Manning had consulted Newman about one of his penitents who was contemplating joining the Roman Catholic Church, and in his reply, dated September 1, 1839, Newman wrote: " I am conscious that we are raising longings and tastes which we are not allowed to supply, and till our bishops and others give scope to the development of Catholicism externally and wisely, we *do* tend to make impatient minds seek it where it has ever been, in Rome. I think that, whenever the time comes that secession to Rome takes place, for which we must not be unprepared, we must boldly say to the Protestant section of our Church: ' *You* are the cause of this. . . . Give us more services, more vestments and decorations in worship; give us monasteries; give us the signs of an apostle, the pledges that the Spouse of Christ is among us. Till then you will have continual secessions to Rome.' "[1] Newman then proceeded to insist that for anyone who did not feel the call to secession an imperative duty, it was a sin. It will be noticed that Newman here insists that the *onus* of responsibility for any secessions that might occur rested with the Protestantism of the leaders of the English Church—a point on which both Pusey and Newman laid great emphasis later.

[1] Purcell, *Life of Manning* i. 233.

We must pass over here the year 1840 and proceed to consider what happened in the beginning of 1841. At the end of February of that year *Tract No.* 90 appeared. It cannot be too strongly emphasized that this *Tract* was conceived and written to deal with the situation which the Romanizing party had created. Herein is probably to be found the reason why Newman was so totally unprepared for the reception of the *Tract* by the wider public. While preparing the *Tract*, Newman was thinking first of the impression which it would make upon the Romanizers, and secondly of the internal dissensions within the Anglo-Catholic party which it would reveal to the world at large. That it was a document which would create a sensation because it revealed his *own* Romanizing tendencies hardly entered his head. The *Tract* was published on February 27, 1841, and a few days later the crash came.

It is unnecessary to recall here the history of the events which in quick succession followed the publication of this pamphlet; they have often been recounted. We must content ourselves with a few references to its contents. The Romanizers were beginning to ask how far it was possible to hold current Roman Catholic teaching in the Church of England. They wished to hold as much of it as possible and they were troubled by the Thirty-nine Articles. Were not these articles inescapably Protestant—the Protestant counterpart to the Catholic Tridentine Canons? The object of *Tract No.* 90 was to prove the converse and to show that some even of the Articles which were thought to be most Protestant were really compatible with sound Catholic teaching. Newman contended that so far from the Articles being directed, as was popularly supposed, specifically against the teaching of the Tridentine Canons, many of them were drawn up at a date prior to that at which the corresponding Canons of the Council of Trent were promulgated. Taken as a whole, the Articles did not aim at repudiating the teachings of the Council. Consequently, if Ward and his friends wished to hold many of the teachings promulgated at Trent, they could do so and still remain members of the Church of England. There were no grounds for secession on this count.

That *Tract No.* 90 should have refrained in general from expressions of marked hostility to Rome was only natural in view of the object with which it was composed. Nevertheless, in the section dealing with the Article (xxxvii.) on the Bishop of Rome, Newman expressly emphasized that there were certain definite barriers between us and Rome. Everyone, he said, who did not join the Roman Church must in consistency profess that the Pope has neither jurisdiction nor authority in this land. The power of the Papacy was an evil which God allowed. " The Papacy began in the exertions and passions of man; and what man can make, man can destroy. Its jurisdiction, while it lasted, was ' ordained of God '; when it ceased to be, it ceased to claim our obedience; and it ceased to be at the Reformation. . . .   Bishop is superior to bishop only in rank, not in real power; and the Bishop of Rome, the head of the Catholic world, is not the centre of unity, except as having a primacy of order " (pp. 78 *f.*). But passages such as these were overlooked in the outcry against the *Tract*.

Newman's defence of *Tract No.* 90, published on the

day after the *Tract* had been condemned by the Hebdo-
madal Board, took the form of a *Letter to Dr. R. W. Jelf*.
In it he pointed out that those who had raised the storm
were not those for whom the *Tract* was intended. " That
the *Tract* has been very inexpedient as addressed to
one class of persons [*i.e.*, the conventional English
Churchmen of 1841] is quite certain; but it was meant
for another, and I sincerely think it necessary for them."
One passage which the *Letter* contained must be quoted,
for Newman spoke in it more favourably of Rome than
he had done in his earlier writings. " In truth, there
is at this moment a great progress of the religious mind
of our Church to something deeper and truer than
satisfied the last century. I always have contended,
and will contend, that it is not satisfactorily accounted
for by any particular movements of individuals on a
particular spot. The poets and philosophers of the
age have borne witness to it many years. Those great
names in our literature, Sir Walter Scott, Mr. Words-
worth, Mr. Coleridge, though in different ways and
with essential differences one from another, and perhaps
from any Church system, still all bear witness to it.
Mr. Alexander Knox in Ireland bears a most surprising
witness to it. The system of Mr. Irving is another
witness to it. The age is moving towards something,
and most unhappily the one religious communion
among us which has of late years been practically in
possession of this something is the Church of Rome.
She alone, amid all the errors and evils of her practical
system, has given free scope to the feelings of awe,
mystery, tenderness, reverence, devotedness, and other
feelings which may be especially called Catholic. The
question then is, whether we shall give them up to the

Roman Church or claim them for ourselves, as we well may, by reverting to that older system, which has of late years indeed been superseded, but which has been, and is, quite congenial (to say the least), I should rather say proper and natural, or even necessary to our Church." It is clear that by this date the ideals of Ward and Oakeley had begun to exercise their influence on Newman.

There are, however, other passages in the Letter of a very different character. " As to the present authoritative teaching of the Church of Rome, to judge by what we see of it in public, I think it goes very far indeed to substitute another Gospel for the true one. . . . If there ever was a system which required reformation it is that of Rome at this day, or in other words (as I should call it) Romanism or Popery " (p. 7). Or in the Postscript, inserted loose in the Letter at the last minute, we read: " Those who are immediately about me know that in the interval between the printing and publication of the *Tract* I was engaged in writing some Letters about Romanism in which I spoke of the impossibility of any approach of the English towards the Roman Church, arising out of the present state of the latter."

Pusey was soon led to enter the fray, and he too addressed a Letter to Jelf, which he entitled *The Articles treated on in Tract* 90 *reconsidered and their Interpretation vindicated in a Letter to the Rev. R. W. Jelf, D.D.* He was prepared to go as far as possible in the direction of supporting Newman, and by implication the Romanizers. Passages occur in this letter in which he too speaks more favourably of Rome than had been usual in his earlier writings. " It should ever be borne in mind," he wrote, "that the Church of Rome has, amid her corruptions, continued to be a faithful witness to the saving truths as to the Blessed Trinity, which were denied by the heretics of the early centuries" (p. 23). Again he fully admitted that Rome had real allurements. She "has many sympathies whereby to draw persons to herself. To those who would lean, she offers undoubting guidance; for those who would have certainty, she offers infallibility; for the devout, she has her churches ever open and her frequent public services, her retreats for devotion and contemplation; for the affectionate, she has the memory of the saints of old; for the imaginative, she has a nominal reverence for Antiquity and a visible unity of communion, spread over the whole world, and everywhere professing to teach the same truth. Her theory of unity . . . at once fills the imagination and contents the intellect" (pp. 154 f.).

But, with this recognition of the merits of the Roman Catholic system, Pusey was very explicit in his condemnation of its errors. Thus, with reference to unity on which Rome lays such stress, he wrote: "The visible unity of the Church falls short of what it should be and what we should have hoped; Rome cuts the knot by maintaining that her one Communion is the one Church. Hers is indeed a fearful theory, cutting off at one stroke 90 millions of the Greek Orthodox Church, as well as our own Communion" (p. 155). He expressed in a postscript his horror of the exaltation of the Blessed Virgin in Roman Catholic devotional life. After quoting some passages from St. Alphonso Liguori's *Glories of Mary*, he concluded: "Whilst these things are so, although we did not separate from Rome, yet since God has permitted that Rome should separate us from her, we see not how the Anglican Church could re-unite with her, without betraying the trust which she owes to her children " (p. 217).

A second pamphlet from Pusey's pen—and it must be remembered that Pusey's pamphlets, like his sermons, were theological treatises, often extending to several hundred pages—appeared in 1842. This took the form of a Letter to his Metropolitan, and was entitled *On Some Circumstances connected with the Present Crisis in the English Church.* By this date Pusey had become fully aware of the attractions which Rome was exercising upon the younger members of the party, and perceived that secession was a real danger. Like ourselves, he wrote, Rome was experiencing a religious awakening. " The Roman Church also has, in some countries certainly, partaken of the same refreshing dew as ourselves; the same Hand, which has touched us, and bid our sleeping Church ' Awake, arise,' has reached her also " (p. 8). Accordingly, the Roman Church in England comes to certain persons " in a fascinating and imposing form " (p. 9).

Pusey insisted that the continual accusations of Popery were the source of grievous harm to such minds. " The very clamour against ' Popery,' within or without the Church, is everywhere tempting persons' curiosity and enlisting their sympathies; they who know nothing about the *Tracts* have had their thoughts turned to Rome, and are interested in her, and study the works of Roman controversialists." And Pusey proceeded to ask the highly relevant question: " If they become bewildered, who should bear the blame— they who inculcate the use of ' Private Judgment ' or

they who would restrain it? they who enjoin obedience
to the Church which has succession from the Apostles,
or they who set the individual's judgment as to Holy
Scripture above the authority of the Church?"
(pp. 31 f.).

In this pamphlet, for the first time in Pusey's writings,
there loomed on the horizon the vision of corporate
reunion with Rome. In a passage which anticipated
his later *Eirenicons*, Pusey expressed an earnest longing
for unity. "The tendency to Romanism, itself but
one phenomenon in the manifold workings of this
eventful day, is, as a whole, but a fruit of the deep
yearning of the stirred Church to be again what her
Saviour left her, One. Our severed members are being
drawn to ourselves, as a Church, and knit into one in
us; as a Church, we are being drawn to other Churches,
that, in God's good time, the whole body may be knit
together under its One Head. Any deep view of the
Church as one whole must create a longing to realize
what, as in vision, it beholds. Our severed state is a
maimed and imperfect condition, checking, we must
fear, the full flow of That Holy Spirit through our
disjointed portions, Which, when perfectly present,
makes what He pervades wholly one, even as He is
the Unity of the Father and the Son. To feel what
the Church should be is to long that it be so. And if
we come not with subdued hearts, settled to wait
God's time for His gift and anxious to take no step
but just where He leads, there must be risk that persons
will seek unity in unallowed ways of their own, and,
as formerly with Dissent, so now in that communion
which embraces the largest portion of Christendom,
and which, in relationship as well as place, is nearest

to us.   This longing must be directed; it cannot, ought
not to, be quenched; yet while it is active (not to speak
of other agents) it were idle to think that any censure
or silencing of men or books can stay what is the result
of implanted sympathies, at the very centre of Christian
life and love " (pp. 25 *f.*).

Passages such as these make it clear that from 1840
onwards the Tractarians used more temperate language
about Rome in order to hinder secessions.   But in
Pusey—and he is representative of those who continued
faithful to the Church of England—it is no question of
any change of principle.

CHAPTER XI

SUMMARY

THE results of our study may be summarized briefly as follows:

The Oxford Movement began in 1833 in order to preserve the Church of England from the dangers which were gathering around her on every side. She had lost her ancient prestige in the eyes of the nation and her principles were being challenged and threatened, not only by the forces of secularism, but also by those of both Dissent and Roman Catholicism. To meet these grave dangers, the *Tracts for the Times Against Popery and Dissent* were begun. Their theological appeal was to the great Anglican divines of the Seventeenth Century, and through them to the Fathers of Antiquity. The original Tractarians had no pro-Roman leanings. So far from seeking to bring the Church of England into closer conformity with Rome, they consistently and constantly engaged in anti-Roman polemic. The high-water mark of the theology of the Movement was Newman's *Lectures on the Prophetical Office of the Church*, issued in 1837; this was a series of lectures which explicitly dealt with the Roman issue.

In 1838 a new stage was reached in the history of the Movement. It was heralded by a number of men of quite different ideals from those of the original Tractarians joining it. Chief among them were two Fellows of Balliol, W. G. Ward and Frederick Oakeley; and these men had their eyes turned Romewards almost from the beginning of their connexion with the Movement. They looked to Rome as their ideal, and sought to introduce Roman Catholic doctrines and practices into the Church of England. Of this group nearly all found their way ultimately into the Roman Catholic Church; but they were no part of the original Movement. The fullest elaboration of their attitude is to be found in Ward's *Ideal of a Christian Church*, which was published in 1844.

This group was not without its effect upon the older Tractarians. It led many of them to speak more temperately of Rome, though this change of language was in most cases occasioned, it would seem, more by considerations of expediency than by any change in conviction. At a time when the Movement was becoming more unpopular every day, and the danger of secessions was ever increasing, the leaders naturally did not wish to reveal the internal rifts within their own ranks.

Newman himself, however, fell under the influence of the new disciples. In 1839 his initial doubts on the Catholicity of the English Church were aroused; and after the *Tract No.* 90 affair of 1841 they became serious. Certainly, from 1841 onwards, Newman did gradually approximate towards Rome until his reception on October 9, 1845.

www.ingramcontent.com/pod-product-compliance
Lightning Source LLC
Chambersburg PA
CBHW062025040426
42447CB00010B/2136